PURGATORY

Moreno Dal Bello

PURGATORY

"In every system...except that of the Bible, the doctrine of a purgatory after death, and prayers for the dead, has always been found to occupy a place. Go wherever we may, in ancient or modern times, we shall find that paganism leaves hope after death for sinners..." **Alexander Hislop**

WHAT IS PURGATORY?

Purgatory! The word itself comes from the old French *purgatoire,* from medieval Latin *purgatorium,* literally: *place of cleansing.* According to the Roman Catholic Catechism, issued with episcopal authority on the occasion of the 4th Plenary Council in 1937, purgatory is *"...a place or state of punishment in the next life where some souls have to suffer for a time, because they are not yet fit to go to heaven."*[1]

Purgatory is sometimes referred to as *God's hospital for souls*, a place where people are healed of their sin before being able to go 'home' to heaven.

The Roman Catholic Church teaches that purgatorial sufferings vary greatly in intensity according to the degree of sinfulness on the part of the sinner. For some the torment will be light and mild, lasting perhaps a few hours. For others, however, the pain is no less than that of hell and can last for several thousand years.

Bellarmine, a noted Roman Catholic theologian, once stated that *"The pains of Purgatory are very severe, surpassing anything endured in this life."*

The Manual of the Purgatorial Society, with the imprimatur of Cardinal Hayes—the imprimatur, along with the 'nihil obstat,' is an official declaration that a book or pamphlet is free, according to the Roman Catholic Church, of doctrinal or moral error—says: *"According to the Holy Fathers of the Church, the fire of Purgatory does not differ from the fire of hell, except in point of duration." "It is the same fire"* says St. Thomas Aquinas, *"that torments the reprobate in hell, and the just in Purgatory. The least pain in Purgatory"* he says, *"surpasses the greatest suffering in this life. Nothing but the eternal duration makes the fire of hell more terrible than that of Purgatory."*[2]

Romanism teaches that although *eternal* punishment may be cancelled through the sacrament of baptism—which the Roman Catholic Church wrongly teaches cleanses a person from original sin—*The Catholic Encyclopedia* points out that, *"...there still remains the temporal punishment required by Divine justice, and this requirement must be fulfilled either in the present life or in the world to come, i.e., in Purgatory. An indulgence offers the penitent sinner the means of discharging this debt during this life on earth."*[3]

The Council of Trent has decreed: *"If you dare to say that a repentant sinner who has been justified by grace is forgiven to such an extent that that person is no longer under an obligation to suffer for his or her sins either here and/or in Purgatory anathema to you!"* (Appen. A, note 2, *A Woman Rides The Beast*).

Roman Catholicism teaches that temporal punishment in Purgatory may be reduced and eventually cancelled by works of penance, by almsgiving, by indulgences and by **paying the priest** to say a mass.

A statement which appears in 'Vatican II – The Conciliar and Post Conciliar Documents' reads, *"The* (Roman) *Church offers the Paschal Sacrifice (the Mass), for the dead so that the dead may be helped by the prayers..."*

Loraine Boettner, author of the classic book *Roman Catholicism*, concludes: *"The doctrine of Purgatory rests on the assumption that while God forgives sin, His justice nevertheless demands that the sinner must suffer the full punishment due to him for his sin before he will be allowed to enter heaven. But such a distinction is illogical...isn't it?...For it manifestly would be unjust to forgive a criminal the guilt of his crime and yet still send him to prison to suffer for it."*[4]

How can a sinner whose sins have been fully atoned for by Christ through His death on the cross, thereby satisfying God's Justice, be required to undergo **any** punishment for said sins, be it permanently or even temporarily, when it is Christ Himself Who, as their Substitute, has had their sins charged to Him and has **fully** paid the price that those sins incurred? Such teaching, along with the lies of every cult concerning the cross of Christ, is a denial of the all sufficiency of

Christ's precious atoning blood to fully wash away the sins of all the people God chose before the foundation of the world. By His death, Jesus Christ has appeased the wrath of God towards all those people God gave to Him, thus **"...making peace by the blood of His cross"** (Colossians 1:20). The apostle Paul continues his letter to the saved people at Colossae, saying that they are **"...now reconciled in His fleshly Body through His death, to present you** (the saved and justified sinner) **HOLY, WITHOUT BLEMISH, and IRREPROACHABLE before Him"** (Colossians 1:22). How can it be thought for one moment that people who are presented to God as holy, without blemish and completely irreproachable, must suffer for their sin before entering heaven. **Isn't it obvious from the above verses and the following verse that the man for whom Christ has died has had the punishment due unto his sins paid for IN FULL by Jesus Christ!** The people for whom Christ died **"...have been consecrated through the offering of the body of Jesus Christ once for all"** (Hebrews 10:10). By the blood of His cross, through His death and through the offering of the body of Jesus Christ peace is established between God and a man, and that man is presented holy, without blemish and irreproachable before God and is consecrated. **What could possibly be required for the justification of a man that Christ Jesus has not obtained?** It is clear from these three verses of Scripture that there is **ABSOLUTELY NO**

PUNISHMENT WHATSOEVER awaiting any for whom Christ shed His blood!!

<u>INDULGENCES</u>

As we have just learned, the Roman Catholic Church teaches that people in Purgatory may be helped by having their time there shortened through the prayers and good works of those on earth. This is done by gaining what is called 'Indulgences' for them, especially through the *'Holy sacrifice of the Mass'*. These Masses are not freely performed but must be <u>paid for</u> by those who request them.

The Roman Catholic Catechism teaches that an Indulgence *"...is a remission, through the power of the* (Roman Catholic) *Church, of the temporal punishment due to sin, after the sin itself has been forgiven."*[5]

In contrast to this the Scriptures state clearly that ***"...without the shedding of blood there is no forgiveness"*** (Hebrews 9:22).

The *buying* of indulgences is encouraged as a way to free souls from Purgatory. In 16th century Germany, one Roman Catholic Church-appointed 'indulgence seller', **John Tetzel**, had a statement written on his collection box, *'As soon as the money in the casket rings, the troubled soul from Purgatory springs.'* I would ask one question of Mr Tetzel: 'How did he know?' It would appear, according to Mr. Tetzel and the Roman Catholic Church, that Christ need not have died to save a sinner from the punishment due unto his sin, but that a mere few coins given into the hand of Rome is all that is required!

In contrast to this nonsense, the Apostle Peter in 1 Peter 1:18,19 states clearly that those whom God has given unto His Son to save were ***"...ransomed... NOT with perishable things like <u>silver or gold</u> but with the <u>precious blood of Christ</u> as of a spotless unblemished lamb."*** We see from this statement that a person CANNOT be ransomed (redeemed) by silver or gold—this includes money payed to the Roman Catholic Church or to anyone else for that matter—but ONLY by the precious blood of Jesus Christ can any man be redeemed. This Scripture quoted directly from the Roman Catholic Bible effectively cancels out the whole concept or need for indulgences! The Old Testament has this to say on the matter of self-redemption by payment of money: ***"One cannot redeem oneself, pay to God a ransom. Too high the price to redeem a life; one would never have enough to stay alive forever and never see the pit...But GOD will redeem my life..."*** (Psalm 49:8-10,16).

"Those who die without anyone to pay for Masses on their behalf are called the 'forgotten souls in Purgatory.' However, these 'forgotten souls' are remembered in special prayers on November 2, known as 'All Soul's Day.' If a Roman Catholic fears he might become one of the forgotten souls, he may join the Purgatorian Society which was established in 1856. A <u>contribution</u> each year to the society will assure him that, upon his death, prayers will be said for

his soul."[6] In line with the ways of this world, it appears that even escaping the fires of punishment for sin, according to Romanism, requires our hard-earned cash!

Even Popes who died up to 500 years ago left vast amounts of riches in order that Masses might be said for them, thus ensuring, to their minds, their eventual release from Purgatory!

It is taught that the Roman Catholic Church herself has power to grant indulgences, which are gained *"...by saying the prayers or by doing the works prescribed by the Church."*[7] Vatican II states: *"The Church...teaches and commands that the usage of indulgences—a usage most beneficial to Christians and approved by the authority of the sacred councils—should be kept in the church, and it condemns with anathema those who say that indulgences are useless or that the church does not have the power to grant them."* (ch. 13, note 1, *A Woman Rides the Beast*).

Romanism also teaches that it is the prerogative of the Pope, as Christ's representative on earth, to grant this relief from suffering **AS HE SEES FIT!** This 'power' to release those in Purgatory became part of the priest's ordination during the 11th century. The fact is, however, that Roman Catholic priests admit that they do not have ANY WAY OF KNOWING when a soul is actually 'released' from Purgatory.

Dr. Charles Hodge reports that the *"Franciscans claimed that the head of their order <u>descended annually into Purgatory,</u> and delivered all the brotherhood that were detained there."*[8]

Ralph Woodrow concludes: *"It is indeed sad that multitudes of people have been deceived into believing that ...the payment of large sums of money, or human works, can pay for their sins.'* The good news is that the price of sin for all God's chosen people has ALREADY BEEN PAID—BY JESUS CHRIST! *"Salvation is by grace—by favor that could never be merited by money, human works or sacrifices."*[9] ***"For by grace you have been saved through faith, and this is <u>not from you</u>; it is the gift of God; IT IS NOT FROM WORKS, so no one may boast"*** (Ephesians 2:8,9).

<u>WHO GOES TO PURGATORY?</u>

Almost all Roman Catholics, according to the Roman Catholic Church, can expect to go to Purgatory after death in order that they might eventually become pure enough to enter heaven. The Church of Rome teaches that there is no salvation AT ALL for those *outside* of the Roman Catholic Church, for those who are not members. Romanism teaches that if a man dies in mortal sin (so called because it is said to kill the soul), he is lost *"...forever in hell"*. However those who die in what is called 'venial' sin, which according to the Roman Catholic Catechism is *"...breaking God's law in a less serious way than by mortal sin"*[10] , go to Purgatory for a time.

Article 98 of the Roman Catechism states that *"...those who die in venial sin, and those who have not done sufficient penance for sin forgiven, are sent to Purgatory."[11]* **It is truly astonishing to note that Romanism says that some degree of punishment remains for the Roman Catholic, even for sins forgiven!!** This teaching is in such contradiction with the Scriptures as to beggar belief that anyone in their right mind could actually believe it!!

Exalted saints and others such as Mary and Roman Catholic martyrs, whose deaths 'brought honour upon the Roman Catholic Church', are said to have escaped Purgatory. Their deaths are considered 'adequate substitutes' for the sufferings of Purgatory, though even in these rare cases no one can be certain that a soul has gone directly to heaven. Purgatory is a mystery; a mystery which causes many to live in a state of constant and hopeless fear, a needless fear which dreads the approaching and inevitable, though fictional, fires of Purgatory. **Though the fires of Purgatory are purely fiction, the fire of Hell is not and it is this eternal fire which awaits all those who do not obey the Gospel of God** (see 2 Thessalonians 1:7-9).

THE ORIGIN AND HISTORY OF PURGATORY

The doctrine of Purgatory evolved from an ancient teaching prevalent among the people of India and Persia, who believed in the concept of a **purification by fire** after death.

This teaching was also prominent amongst the Egyptians, as well as the Greeks and Romans. The Greeks' influence reached as far as Palestine, where gradually the Rabbis began to teach that sin offerings made by children could relieve their deceased parents of great suffering.

Even the ancient philosopher **Plato** (427-347 B.C.), accepted the concept that a perfect happiness was unattainable after one's death until one had atoned for one's sins through suffering the pains of a purifying fire. Such teaching does away with any thought of an atoning death of a Savior for His people. Notably, the worst of sinners, according to **Plato**, would suffer eternally. This totally anti-christian and unbiblical view to which **Plato** subscribed is **fully supported and maintained by the Roman Catholic Church and presented to YOU, the Roman Catholic, as Christian teaching!**

Also of interest is the fact that **Plato** spoke of the Orphic teachers of his day, who belonged to a mystery religion of ancient Greece, *"Who flock to the rich man's doors and try to persuade him that they have <u>a power at their command, which they procure from heaven</u>, and which enables them by sacrifices and incantation...to make amends for any crime committed by the individual himself, or his ancestors....<u>Their mysteries deliver us of the other world</u>, while the neglect of them is punished by an awful doom."*[12] It really should come as no surprise that the claims made by Roman Catholicism are identical to those of **Plato** and the pagan priests of Orphism.

Devotees of Zoroastrianism, a pagan religion which can be traced as far back as 3,000 B.C., did not believe in an eternal hell, but in a temporary place of suffering for the **purposes of correction.** It was taught that these souls proceeded through twelve different stages of punishment before being sufficiently purified to enter heaven.

The Stoics, believers in an ancient form of Greek philosophy, held the idea of a 'middle place' of enlightenment which they named 'Empurosis', meaning **'a place of fire'**.

It is abundantly clear from all the evidence presented thus far, that the concept of a purgatorial fire, a fire said to purify and cleanse a man of his sins, has existed for centuries in the natural, unregenerate mind of *pagan* man throughout the world and has merely been incorporated into the teachings of the Roman Catholic Church.

Oddly, in light of Roman Catholicism's insistence that Purgatory is a biblical teaching, the whole concept of temporal punishment for the purposes of purification was not introduced into the Roman Catholic Church until the end of the 6th century, when Pope Gregory the Great proclaimed that as well as heaven and hell, there existed a *third state*, a place where souls could be purified before being admitted into heaven. Even more peculiar is the fact that this papal ruling was not sanctioned by the Roman Catholic Church as official dogma until the Council of Florence in 1439 and was later confirmed by the Council of Trent in 1548.

Loraine Boettner poses the following question, *"...Does any intelligent person really* *believe in their heart of hearts that if such a place as purgatory were included in the pages of the Bible it would have taken the church fathers 600 years to discover it, and another 1000 years to confirm it?"*[13]

It is reported that the theologian **St. Augustine** once positively stated that nobody was obliged to believe in Purgatory. **Charles Chiniquy**, former Roman Catholic priest and author of the revealing book *50 Years in the 'Church' of Rome*, has commented, *"Several of the fathers consider purgatory as of pagan origin.* ***Tertullian*** *spoke of it only after he had joined the sect of the Montanists (a heretical cult of the 2nd century), and he confesses that it is* <u>*not through the Holy Scriptures*</u>*, but through the inspiration of the Paraclete of Montanus that he knows anything about purgatory. Augustine, the most learned and pious of the holy fathers, does not find purgatory in the Bible, and positively says that* <u>*its existence is dubious*</u>*.*"[14]

In his assessment of the doctrine of Purgatory and its effects on the Roman Catholic, **Dr. Laird R. Harris** states: *"It is well to remember that the doctrine of Purgatory which rests like a heavy burden upon the heart of every Roman Catholic was* <u>*not taught by any of the early church fathers*</u> *and had a very slow growth until the fifth century. Its beginnings in prayers for the dead and a difference in status between the martyred dead and the ordinary Christian departed may be found as early as 200 A.D. in the writings of Tertullian. Mention of the* <u>*penal fires*</u>

comes much later, and the masses for the poor souls in purgatory still later. The doctrine of Purgatory is another one of those foreign growths that has fastened itself like a malignant tumor upon the theology of the Roman Catholic Church."[15]

ROMAN CATHOLIC 'EVIDENCE' OF PURGATORY

Four Scripture passages are commonly referred to by the Roman Catholic Church in support of their doctrine of Purgatory: Matthew 3:11; 1 Corinthians 3:15; 1 Peter 3:18-20; and Jude 22,23. Despite their being implemented by Rome, none of these Scriptures mention Purgatory at all. The only other writings which the Roman Catholic Church has appealed to concerning Purgatory and prayers for the dead, are to be found in the Apocrypha, a set of 15 books considered by the Roman Church as Holy Scripture, and which **must** be accepted by **all** Roman Catholics as Holy Scripture under penalty of mortal sin!

The Apocrypha has, to this day, NEVER been received by the Jews as being divinely inspired of God, and has always been rejected as such. Oddly, the Council of Trent in 1546, pronounced, *"We receive as Old Testament books only those books which have always been held to be divinely inspired, by the Jews."* The Council of Trent then, inexplicably and in complete contradiction to the above statement, promptly added the Apocrypha to the list of Old Testament books almost 2,000 years after the completion of the Old Testament, with several members of the Council opposing the move. Even today opinion is divided within the Roman Catholic Church as to whether the Apocrypha is inspired.

The New Testament includes about 260 direct quotations and approximately 320 allusions to the Old Testament, yet **not once** is mention made of a single verse found in the Apocrypha!

One of these apocryphal books is called 2 Maccabees, a Jewish book written after the closure of the Old Testament, which has for centuries been used by the Roman Catholic Church to confirm her teachings on Purgatory and prayers for the dead. The passage in question is 2 Maccabees 12:39-46, a flimsy passage, to say the least, on which to base a doctrine that plays such an integral part in Roman Catholic theology.

The dependability of the passage has diminished significantly, as we see in the official Roman Catholic Church approved footnotes to verses 42-46 from the Roman Catholic Bible, that what is spoken of in the passage is *"...similar to, but <u>not quite the same as</u>, the (Roman) Catholic doctrine of Purgatory."*

No mention is made in the passage of *Purgatory* or *fire* or even of *tormented souls*. All that is spoken of is prayers for the dead, which Roman Catholic theologians mistakenly believe can be effective for the salvation of the dead. Yet Bible believing Christians know that the Bible says, ***"It is appointed that human beings die once, and after this the JUDGEMENT"***

(Hebrews 9:27). Praying for the dead, according to the Roman Catholic Bible, is not only heretical but a complete waste of time, for a man lives once and is then judged according to that life and not upon any prayers for the deceased person.

Loraine Boettner points out that *"...from the Roman Catholic viewpoint, these verses prove too much, for they teach the possible salvation of soldiers who had died in mortal sin, that of idolatry. And that contradicts Roman Catholic doctrine, which is that those dying in mortal sin go straight to hell and are PERMANENTLY LOST. They do not go to purgatory where they can be aided by the prayers of people still on earth."*[16]

What may come as quite a surprise to Roman Catholics is the fact that many Roman Catholic theologians now reject the 2 Maccabees passage as proof of the existence of Purgatory. For most, the mere fact that the Pope has said it exists is proof enough! The question every Roman Catholic must ask themselves is: 'How reliable can this teaching of Purgatory be, when the **principle passage** used for centuries as proof of its existence is now **rejected?**'

WHAT DOES THE ROMAN CATHOLIC BIBLE SAY?

Nowhere in the Roman Catholic Bible is there ANY reference made WHATSOEVER to a temporary place of punishment such as purgatory, where sin is atoned for. What may startle many Roman

Catholics is the fact that the Roman Catholic Church **readily admits to this!**

The *Roman Catholic Dictionary* of 1928, p.704, says, *"We would appeal to those general principles of Scripture, <u>rather than to particular texts</u> often alleged in proof of Purgatory. WE DOUBT IF THEY CONTAIN ANY EXPLICIT AND DIRECT REFERENCE TO IT."* It is a fact that can be stated with the utmost confidence: **Purgatory does not exist, either in reality or in the pages of the Roman Catholic Bible!**

The Roman Catholic teaching of Purgatory flies directly in the face of sound Bible doctrine which **assures** the true believer of salvation; of being immediately with the Lord when absent from the body. 1 John 5:13 says, ***"I write these things to you so that you may KNOW that you HAVE eternal life, you who believe in the name of the Son of God."*** Scripture also states emphatically that ***"...now there is NO CONDEMNATION for those who are in Christ Jesus"*** (Romans 8:1). **How then can anyone even conceive the possibility that any form of punishment now awaits those whom not even God has any condemnation towards?** ***"Who will bring a charge against God's chosen ones? It is God Who acquits us"*** (Romans 8:33).

We shall now present several other Scriptures from the Roman Catholic Bible which clearly demonstrate that the true Christian does not suffer in any 'Purgatory', because punishment due unto their sin has been **PAID IN FULL BY THE LORD JESUS CHRIST:**

* John 5:24 - **"...whoever hears My Word and believes in the One who sent Me HAS ETERNAL LIFE AND <u>WILL NOT COME TO CONDEMNATION</u> BUT HAS PASSED FROM DEATH TO LIFE."**

* Hebrews 10:10 - **"...WE HAVE BEEN CONSECRATED through the offering of the body of Jesus Christ ONCE FOR ALL."**

* 1 John 1:7- **"...and the BLOOD of His Son Jesus Christ CLEANSES US FROM ALL SIN."**

Many other Bible texts also shatter the myth of Purgatory. Firstly, Jesus Christ said plainly to the penitent thief, **"...TODAY you will be with Me in PARADISE"** (Luke 23:43). These words of Jesus show clearly that both He and the thief went **THAT DAY** to Paradise, and not to the tormenting fires of a fabled Purgatory.

Luke 16:19-31 is the passage where Jesus tells of the destiny of two men after they had suffered death. Verse 22 says: **"When the poor man died, he was carried away by angels TO THE BOSOM OF ABRAHAM. The rich man also died and was buried."** Later in verse 23, the rich man spoke **"...from the <u>netherworld</u> where he was in torment..."** The Greek word in the original text for netherworld is *had s*, which is a place of torment and detention for lost souls until the Judgement Day when, according to Revelation 20, hades and its inhabitants will be thrown into the Lake of Fire, the *eternal* place of torment.

Moreover Abraham, speaking to the rich man in hades in v.26 of Luke 16 states: ***"...between us and you a great chasm is established to prevent anyone from crossing who might wish to go from our side to yours or from your side to ours."*** It is patently obvious from these Scriptures that people who are in hades are there PERMANENTLY until they are judged and thrown into the Lake of Fire (Revelation 20:12-15). This precludes any possibility that hades may be the Purgatory which Roman Catholics have been taught. For hades is a place of **punishment, not purification** and none who are in it will ever escape God's Wrath but will eventually be thrown into the Lake of Fire, the place of everlasting fire and torment.

1 Corinthians 11:32 sees the apostle Paul speaking of the Lord lovingly *disciplining* His people <u>on earth</u> ***"...so that we may not be <u>condemned</u> along with the world."*** Again, Paul also mentions in Romans 8:1 that ***"...NOW THERE IS NO CONDEMNATION FOR THOSE WHO ARE IN CHRIST JESUS."*** If, then, there is no condemnation for the true believer, it stands to biblical reason that there cannot be a Purgatory awaiting him! If there is no condemnation, then it is biblically logical to conclude that there is no punishment awaiting the justified believer when he departs this life.

The words of Jesus uttered upon the cursed tree, **"It is finished"** (John 19:30), speak of the completion of the work of redemption. Sin has been paid for IN FULL by the Lord Jesus Christ. **Jesus took all the pain of the cross so that His people would not have to endure one moment of punishment for their sins, eternal or temporary!!**

Speaking of the Christ, the prophet Isaiah wrote of God's people: **"...it was our infirmities that He bore, our sufferings that He endured....He was pierced for our offences, crushed for our sins, <u>upon Him was the chastisement that makes us whole</u>, by His stripes we were healed....the Lord laid upon Him the guilt of us all....smitten for the sin of His people"**. God states that **"...through <u>His suffering</u>, My Servant shall justify many, and their guilt He shall bear....He shall take away the sins of many, and win pardon for their offences"** (Isaiah 53:4-6,8,11,12). I defy anyone, in the face of such convincing Scriptural evidence as this, to say that there remains the slightest condemnation or punishment for sin of any of those for whom Christ Jesus the Lord died! **What possible punishment remains for those whose very guilt was borne, and whose sins have been taken away, by the Savior and for whom a FULL PARDON HAS BEEN WON!!**

The apostle Paul, in the following verses, confirms the truth that the true Christian goes directly to heaven to be with God when he dies: Paul says, **"...and we would rather leave the**

body and go home to the Lord" (2 Corinthians 5:8) and in Philippians 1:23, ***"...I long to depart this life and be with Christ, (for) that is far better."*** Paul, as well as every other writer of the New Testament, and Old, never once spoke of Purgatory. **They spoke many times about heaven and hell but NEVER Purgatory.**

And so it becomes perfectly clear, that upon investigation of the Roman Catholic Church's claims of Purgatory, particularly when one engages in a search of the Word of God, that there is no punishment, no need to be purged of sin in the fires of a mythical Purgatory, for the true Christian's sins **HAVE BEEN FULLY PURGED** by the death and resurrection of the Lord Jesus Christ. Hebrews 1:3 states that it is by Christ's death for His people that He has ***"...accomplished purification from sins..."*** Again, how can there be any punishment awaiting those who have been purified, having had their sins purged forever by the Savior Jesus? Revelation 1:5 states: ***"...To Him who loves us and HAS FREED US from our sins BY HIS BLOOD...",*** meaning His physical death. The work of salvation is done; the work of purification HAS BEEN accomplished!

One of the reasons for the Church of Rome having kept the Bible from the people for centuries, and even burning them (a period fitly known as the Dark Ages), is the fact that the Roman Catholic Church is well aware that many of its teachings are just not in the Bible!, one of these being Purgatory. Another reason is the fact that the Bible, the perfect Word of Almighty God, totally exposes and condemns the unbiblical teachings and pagan practices of Roman Catholicism. Although the Roman Catholic Church now advocates the reading of the Bible, one must receive the interpretation solely from her. In other words, like any cult she says, 'Read the Scriptures as much as you like but believe only what WE teach the Bible says.'

CHRIST'S ATONING SACRIFICE - INSUFFICIENT?

The most serious consequence of the doctrine of Purgatory is the fact that it denies the sufficiency and efficiency of the blood of Christ—that is His death—to fully atone for the sins of all for whom He died.

We have seen that the Roman Catholic concept of Purgatory agrees with that of many pagan nations, in that it is a place of temporary punishment for the purification of sinners by the torments of fire.

Let it be stated quite emphatically that all the fires of hell itself could never burn out one stain of the least of sins!! The fire of hell is no aid to purification, but a means of torment and eternal punishment, a display of the eternal wrath of God against sin. The thinking Roman Catholic must ask himself: 'If there was such a place as Purgatory, why then did Jesus Christ come to the earth to die on the cross? What was His death all about and why was He called *"...the Lamb of God who TAKES AWAY THE SIN OF THE WORLD"* (John 1:29) and, therefore, the punishment due unto that sin? **How can there be any remaining punishment for that which has been taken away?** If Jesus Christ has taken away the sins of those for whom He died, why then would there be reason left for punishment, even a temporary punishment, for Christ's own people, for the wrath of God, which sin has merited, has been fully satisfied by Christ's Bodily sacrifice upon the cross. The following passage links the believer's escaping the wrath of God with the death of the Lord Jesus. Speaking to believers, the apostle Paul stated: *"For God did not destine us for wrath, but to gain salvation through our Lord Jesus Christ, Who died for us..."* (1 Thessalonians 5:9,10).

Roman Catholicism teaches that Jesus Christ died to redeem mankind from its sins, yet simultaneously promotes the idea that there is a need after death for most people to suffer punishment for their sins. Page 206 of the *Baltimore Catechism* states: *"After sin has been healed by the medicine of the sacrament of penance, the wounds left by sin must be healed by the <u>future medicine of temporal punishment</u>."* Notice here that there is no mention of Christ's precious blood, the **ONLY** 'medicine' that can *heal* us of our sins. *"But He was pierced for our offenses, crushed for our sins, upon Him was the chastisement that makes us whole, BY <u>HIS STRIPES</u> WE WERE HEALED"* (Isaiah 53:5).

In complete contrast to this, the Roman Catholic Bible teaches that the Death and Resurrection of the Lord Jesus Christ unequivocally does away with the need for a place of temporal punishment such as Purgatory. Many Scriptures bear this out. Here is just a sample:

* Hebrews 9:26 - ***"...But now once for all He has appeared at the end of the ages to take away sin BY HIS SACRIFICE."***

* Hebrews 10:14 - ***"For by ONE offering HE HAS MADE PERFECT FOREVER..."***

* Hebrews 13:12 - ***"Therefore, Jesus also suffered...to consecrate the people BY HIS OWN BLOOD."*** (Not so that they would become consecrated by the addition of their own suffering) It is plain for all to see that even the Roman Catholic Bible confirms the fact that Jesus Christ, by His sacrificial death upon the tree, by His shed blood, has consecrated His people; He has cleansed the true believer from **all** sin for **all** time and has thus done away with any need for any of them to suffer one moment of punishment for their sins. In taking away from the effectiveness of Christ's blood to wash away sin and from its all sufficiency to achieve what it was poured out for, Roman Catholicism joins hands with every cult and false religion in existence, which have much in common, not the least of which being the perversion of the Bible doctrine of the blood of Christ being the sole means of the full atonement

for the sins of all those for whom it was shed, reducing it to something that is only part of the sin solution.

God's justice has been fully satisfied, as we see from Colossians 2:13,14: ***"And even when you were dead (in) transgressions and the uncircumcision of your flesh, HE BROUGHT YOU TO LIFE ALONG WITH HIM, having forgiven us all our transgressions; OBLITERATING THE BOND AGAINST US, with its legal claims, which was opposed to us, He also removed it from our midst, NAILING IT TO THE CROSS."*** Dear Roman Catholic, the price for the Christian's sin HAS been paid in full!

The Roman Catholic Church is no different to the cults and sects who deny the efficiency of Christ's atoning death upon the tree to cleanse His people from their sin ONCE AND FOR ALL! If you believe in Purgatory, you cannot hold to the truth that Jesus Christ has totally and eternally forgiven the Christian of his sins — **PAST, PRESENT AND FUTURE!**

Likewise, if you believe that Jesus Christ died for your sins, you cannot simultaneously hold to the lie that there exists, or that there is even a need for, such a place as Purgatory. **The doctrine of Purgatory negates the work of Christ on the cross.** It completely nullifies the fact that His death was a substitutionary sacrifice and that all for whom He died are freed from the wrath to come.

The Roman Catholic Bible teaches that blood alone can purify a man from sin. Leviticus

17:11 says, **"...it is the blood, as the seat of life, that makes atonement."** The footnotes to this verse in the Roman Catholic Bible add: *"This idea of sacrifice is applied in Hebrews 9-10 to the death of Christ, inasmuch as,* **'without the shedding of blood there is no forgiveness'"** (Hebrews 9:22). (See also Revelation 7:14.) Many Roman Catholics are under the mistaken belief that they will not suffer the wrath to come because they have suffered enough here on earth. This lie also does away with the need of a Savior and His atoning death upon the cross.

The first part of Hebrews 9:22 says, **"According to law almost everything is purified by blood..."** The only things referred to by the writer as not purified by blood were inanimate objects such as gold and silver, which were purified by fire (see Numbers 31:22,23). But when it came to sins, it was universally true that ONLY BLOOD COULD REDEEM A MAN FROM SIN. The words of author **Wilson Ewin** conclude this chapter: *"...only complete faith in the shed blood of Jesus Christ can satisfy God (Romans 3:25). Christ's blood cleanses from all sin (1 John 1:7,9). There is no further satisfaction to be made (Hebrews 10:18)."*[17]

IN CONCLUSION...

Eventually, according to Roman Catholic dogma, Purgatory will be emptied of its inhabitants. But as we see in Revelation 20:13,14 death, hades and the sea will all give up their dead. There is no mention made of a place called Purgatory.

Loraine Boettner gives his summary on the doctrine of Purgatory by stating: *"We charge in the strongest terms that the practice of saying mass for souls in purgatory is a gigantic hoax and fraud, a taking of money under false pretenses, because it purports to get people out of purgatory when actually no such place exists....Why...should we trust a priest who presents an interpretation concerning the afterlife which is not only not in the Bible but which is contrary to the clear teaching of the Bible? Such practice is fraudulent and is designed primarily for only one purpose, that of keeping the people under the power of the priests and controlling their lives and property as far as possible."*[18]

The sad truth of the doctrine of Purgatory is that it keeps those who believe it to be true in the bondage of fear, with nothing to look forward to at the end of life on earth but the tormenting fires of this imaginary place. **NOT EVEN THE ROMAN CATHOLIC 'SAVIOR' CAN SAVE ANYONE FROM THE FIRES OF PURGATORY!!** The poor Roman Catholic is told that faith **alone** in the atoning work of Christ **alone** to make satisfaction for His people's sins is not enough, but that, in an effort to successfully escape Purgatory, money must be paid to the Roman Catholic Church to secure a place in heaven!

"It is difficult to conceive of a belief so groundless and yet so frightening as that of the doctrine of Purgatory. But what a marvellous,

glorious thing it is at death to go STRAIGHT TO HEAVEN! And what good news it is for Roman Catholics when they learn that there is no such place as Purgatory, no suffering for the <u>redeemed</u> soul beyond the grave!"[19]

We close this chapter with the clearest possible message to you, the Roman Catholic, by quoting, from the Roman Catholic Bible itself, the words of the Lord Jesus Christ as proof that there is no punishment awaiting the true believer after death: ***"AMEN, AMEN, I SAY TO YOU, WHOEVER HEARS MY WORD AND BELIEVES IN THE ONE WHO SENT ME, HAS ETERNAL LIFE AND WILL NOT COME TO CONDEMNATION, BUT HAS PASSED FROM DEATH TO LIFE"*** (John 5:24).

COME OUT FROM HER....

The purpose of this booklet has not been to judge or condemn you, the Roman Catholic, but has been designed to educate you, to inform you of facts and proper biblical teaching which the Roman Catholic Church has not given you. It has been written in order to provide you with historical facts about the origins of many of your Church's teachings and traditions. **You have read for yourself what the Roman Catholic Church admits to and what your own Roman Catholic Bible says, and doesn't say—what it teaches and simply does not support.** Ultimately, this booklet is a plea for you to come out of the Roman Catholic Church, away from all its man-made doctrines and pagan practices, away from its false gospel. **God must be worshipped HIS way, for no other way is acceptable unto Him.** There is no other way to worship the true God—**and therefore be a saved, justified and true follower of God**—other than the way He has prescribed in His Holy Word. **There is no Gospel that must be believed, by which a man is saved, other than the one that reveals the Righteousness of Christ.**

We have presented the truth to you. **Verifiable truth.** We have quoted from many sources approved by your own Church including a Church approved Bible. But do not believe things simply because you saw them written in a booklet. The Bible commends those who properly investigate what is presented to them as truth and we encourage you to do so. In Acts 17:11 the apostle Paul and Silas preached to the people at Berea. The Roman Catholic Bible says that ***"These...were more fair-minded than those in Thessalonica, for they received the word with all willingness and EXAMINED THE SCRIPTURES DAILY TO DETERMINE WHETHER THESE THINGS WERE SO."*** The Scriptures were their sole authority. They did not refer to the writings of mere men, seeking out their opinions, but went immediately to the Holy Word of God **knowing** that His Word alone could be trusted, and was the sure test for all teachings being presented as God's own decrees (see 2 Peter 1:19). Paul and Silas were not offended by their examining and putting to the test what they was saying, they did not say *'How dare you examine what we have said to you; don't you know who we are?'* **Every Christian, indeed every person, is to examine by the Holy Scriptures all that is presented to him as God's teaching, and if it does not match with the Scriptures, you can be sure it did not come from God and is to be rejected out of hand.** Writing to true believers, John said, ***"Beloved, DO NOT TRUST every spirit BUT TEST the spirits to see whether they belong to God, because many false prophets have gone out into the world"*** (1 John 4:1).

The subtle deceptiveness of the Roman Catholic Church is that she teaches some truths of Scripture but always adds to them, something which the Scriptures roundly condemn: ***"Add NOTHING to HIS Words, lest He reprove you, and you be exposed as a deceiver"*** (Proverbs 30:6). In speaking against such deception the Lord Jesus warned His disciples to ***"...Look out, and beware of the leaven of the Pharisees and Sadducees"*** (Matthew 16:6 cf. Galatians 5:9). Later, the disciples ***"...understood that He was not telling them to beware of the leaven of bread, but of THE TEACHING of the Pharisees and Sadducees"*** (Matthew 16:12). The Pharisees and Sadducees were the religious leaders in Jesus' day. The apostle Paul warned: ***"...watch out for those who create dissensions and obstacles, in opposition to the teaching that you learned; avoid them. For such people do not serve our Lord Christ*** *but their own appetites, and by fair and flattering speech they deceive the hearts of the innocent"* (Romans 16:17,18). EXAMINE EVERYTHING! TEST EVERYTHING BY THE WORD OF GOD! **For we are dealing with eternal issues here. We are dealing with heaven and hell, and what a person believes determines their eternal destiny, for the doctrine you hold to is the surest evidence of whether or not it is the true God Who has revealed Himself to you or whether it is a false god whom you have embraced.**

Some examples of such deceptiveness are as follows: the Roman Catholic Church teaches her followers to pray the Lord's prayer, but they are encouraged to do so whilst holding the Rosary which is a pagan invention and has nothing to do with true Christianity. Yes, Rome agrees that God alone forgives sin, but they add that this power to forgive has been given to her priests and one must go *to them* to receive it and not directly to God the Father through Jesus His Son, as the Scriptures prescribe. Yes, Roman Catholicism teaches that the Bible is the Word of God but it considers tradition to be *equal* to God's precious Holy Word and insists that she is the only true interpreter of Scripture! **In other words, what ROME says God's Word is saying is what is to be obeyed, rather than what the Scripture's interpretation of Itself is saying! Compare Scripture with Scripture, not Scripture with a man's interpretation.** All along, Roman Catholicism adds to God's Word and in other instances withholds certain parts of it, such as the second Commandment, from its publications. It is true that Roman Catholicism teaches 'the death, burial and resurrection' of Jesus Christ but it is vitally important to note that while she may correctly teach some aspects of these things—things which are aligned with historical fact—the Roman Catholic Church **does not** teach the death, burial and resurrection of Jesus Christ ***"...in accordance with the Scriptures..."*** (1 Corinthians 15:3,4).

It is no accident that so much pagan tradition is found today in Roman Catholicism. It has been carefully managed and seen to, that old pagan/occultic rites and traditions, which the Bible calls demonic, are continued to be adhered to and promoted as vigilantly as they were by the early pagans, but now with a Christian veneer thus setting up the Roman Catholic Church as the unmistakably identifiable anti-christian system referred to as 'Babylon' in the Bible. Roman Catholicism stands today not only against Christ, for it does not teach His Gospel, but Rome has also, in a most vulgar way, usurped Christ's position. The papacy claims that **it** is the vicar of Christ on earth, rather than the Holy Spirit as the Word of God says.

That which immediately reveals a religious organization's ungodly foundation may be seen in the gospel it teaches. What a person, or organization such as the Roman Catholic Church, says about **Who Jesus Christ is, what He has done and for whom He has done it**—in other words His Person and His Work—will reveal whether or not that person or organization is of God (see 2 John 9). After having preached to them the True and only Gospel of salvation which reveals the true God and true Christ, Paul the apostle warned the believers in Galatia that ***"...even if we or an angel from heaven should preach to you a gospel OTHER THAN the one that we preached to you, let that one be accursed"*** (Galatians 1:8).

There are many who by nature are religious; many who are extremely zealous for what they believe to be the things of God, yet Scripture reminds us that by nature ***"There is no one just, not one, there is no one who understands, there is no one who seeks God"*** (Romans 3:10,11). Saving, God-given faith in the true and only Gospel of God shows that it is the true God Who has revealed Himself. **Belief in any gospel other than that one and only Gospel of God reveals that it is not the true God Who has revealed Himself but rather a false god who cannot save.**

We implore you to come out of the Roman Catholic Church. A Church which is headed, not by the Lord Jesus Christ, for it does not promote His Gospel, but by a man who calls himself the 'Pope', and who allows himself to be addressed as 'Holy Father', a title which God **ALONE** is worthy. God ALONE is Father, and God ALONE is Holy. The Lord Jesus only ever referred to God as 'Father', and in Revelation 15:4 Jesus, praying to the Father said: ***"...You ALONE are Holy..."*** How dare ANY man take upon himself a title of which ONLY God is worthy! Not incidentally, the Lord Jesus Christ also said to His followers not to call any man on earth father, that is in a spiritual sense, for One was their Father and He resides in heaven: ***"Call no one on earth your father; you have but one Father in heaven"*** (Matthew 23:9). Roman Catholicism responds to these words of the Lord Jesus by calling *every one of its priests 'father',* and demanding that everyone else, Roman Catholic or not, do likewise despite admitting in their footnotes to Matthew 23:9 that, *"...Jesus forbids not only the titles (rabbi, father and master) but the spirit of superiority and pride that is shown by their acceptance."*

Pope Leo XIII once blasphemously declared: *"The Pope holds upon this earth the place of God Almighty..."* **Robert Bellermine**, famous Jesuit Cardinal of the 16th century and also a saint of the Roman Catholic Church, had this to say: *"All the names which in the Scriptures are applied to Christ by virtue of which it is established that He is over the Church, all the same names are applied to the Pope."* The *Catholique Nationale* of Paris, in its July 13, 1895 issue, contained the following claim made by the then archbishop of Venice, later to become Pope Pius X. He said, *"The Pope is not only the representative of Jesus Christ, but he is Jesus Christ Himself hidden under the veil of the flesh..."* Dear Roman Catholic, **the Pope is NOT Jesus Christ! JESUS CHRIST IS GOD!! ONLY through the Lord Jesus Christ is there**

salvation, not through the Pope and his 'church' of Rome.

"History is replete with sayings that mocked Romanism's false claim to celibacy: 'The holiest hermit has his whore'" and "'Rome has more prostitutes than any other city because she has the most celibates'" are examples. Pope Pius II called Rome *'The only city run by bastards, the sons and grandsons of popes and cardinals'.*

"Even Roman Catholic historians admit that among the popes were some of the most degenerate and unconscionable ogres in all history. More than one pope was slain by a husband who found him in bed with his wife. To call such a man 'His holiness vicar of Christ' makes a mockery of holiness and Christ. Yet the name of each of these mass murderers, fornicators, robbers, warmongers—some guilty of the massacre of thousands—is emblazoned in honor on the Church's official list of Peter's alleged successors, the popes" ('The Berean Call', July '94, p.2).

"Will you believe the words of the Roman Catholic Church or will you believe the words of the Roman Catholic Bible? It is for you to decide. Remember, there are only two religions in the entire world, man's and God's. If it is not the truth of God that you are believing, then you have embraced the lies of the Devil." **You have embraced a false gospel wherein is no salvation.** *"Man's religion is by works—his own efforts, his fastings and prayers, his obedience to the Church. That, in effect, makes him his own*

saviour. God's is by faith in the finished work of Jesus Christ. Jesus paid it all... The Roman Catholic Bible states clearly: **"...we have been JUSTIFIED BY FAITH, we have peace with God through our Lord Jesus Christ...***Romans 5:1."* *The Roman Catholic Bible makes it perfectly clear that man cannot save himself and that Christ is his only hope; his only Saviour."*[20]

"Salvation is not dependent on a human priest, Mary, Baptism, the saints, the sacraments, the Mass, confession, good works, membership in the Roman Catholic Church or the Pope."

Salvation is not gained by our loyalty or service to a person—**be they our parents or grandparents and their religious traditions which they have passed down to us**—or to an institution such as the Roman Catholic Church, but rather by our **acceptance of the truth**!! *"Jesus said:* **"...I am the Way and the Truth and the Life. No one comes to the Father EXCEPT THROUGH ME"** *(John 14:6)* and **"I am the Gate. Whoever enters through Me will be saved..."** (John 10:9). *Acts 4:12 says:* **'There is NO salvation through ANYONE else, nor is there ANY other name under heaven given to the human race by which we are to be saved.'**

It matters not how religious a person is or how sincere he might be in his religious pursuits, if a man has not the Gospel of God, if he does not **"...remain in the teaching of the Christ** (he) **does not have God..."** (2 John 9). **"That all who have not believed the truth but have approved wrongdoing may be condemned"**

(2 Thessalonians 2:12). Scripture also speaks of the vengeance that will be had upon the enemies of God *"...at the revelation of the Lord Jesus from heaven with His mighty angels, in blazing fire, inflicting punishment on those who do not acknowledge God and on those WHO DO NOT OBEY THE GOSPEL of our Lord Jesus. These will pay the penalty of eternal ruin, separated from the presence of the Lord and from the glory of His power"* (1 Thessalonians 7-9).

Only through the Gospel of Christ wherein is revealed the Righteousness of Christ, without which no man can be saved, is there true salvation: *"For I am not ashamed of the Gospel. IT IS THE POWER OF GOD for the salvation of everyone who believes: for the Jew first, and then Greek. For in it is revealed the Righteousness of God from faith to faith; as it is written, the one who is righteous __by faith__ will live"* (Romans 1:16,17). Central to the Gospel message is the Person and Work of Jesus Christ and, according to the Scriptures, if one is wrong about Christ, if one has embraced erroneous doctrine concerning Christ the Person and His Work, one is not merely in need of correction yet nevertheless saved, one has in fact fallen for another jesus who is identified by false doctrine, and thus remains in a lost state. **Only in the True Jesus is their salvation. Belief, however sincere, in a false jesus CANNOT SAVE!** You see, not only does the apostle Paul state that the Gospel is the power of God but he also defines this statement in 1 Corinthians 1:18: ***"THE MESSAGE OF THE CROSS is foolishness to those who are perishing, but to us who are being saved IT*** (THE CROSS) ***IS THE POWER OF GOD."***

Belief in false doctrines concerning Christ constitutes a belief in *another* gospel, one which does not represent the true Christ but a false savior (see 2 Corinthians 11:3,4). The Holy Spirit is the Spirit of Truth (John 14:17; 15:26; 16:13) and never presents a man with, nor leads him to believe, a false gospel: ***"But when He comes, the Spirit of Truth, He will guide you to all truth..."*** (John 16:13). Jesus prayed, ***"Consecrate them in the Truth. Your Word is Truth"*** (John 17:17). The true believer is consecrated, or sanctified, through the truth which is the Word of God and not through the lies of men. Speaking to saved men, the apostle Paul stated: ***"...God chose you as the firstfruits for salvation through sanctification BY THE SPIRIT AND BELIEF IN TRUTH"*** (2 Thessalonians 2:13). There is no true sanctification if one's faith is not in the Truth of God.

Only by belief in Christ's Gospel, which says that man is dead in sin, without God and without hope of salvation by anything he is or does in an effort to please God and gain His favor, is a man saved: ***"Therefore, remember that at one time you...were at that time without Christ...without hope and without God in the world"*** (Ephesians 2:11-13). ***"You were dead in***

your transgressions and sins"* (Ephesians 2:1). ***"All have sinned and are deprived of the glory of God"*** (Romans 3:23).

Only by belief in Christ's Gospel, which says that a man is saved not by works, not by anything he has done, is doing or will do, but solely by the grace and mercy of God, is a man saved: ***"...a person is not justified by works of the law but through faith in Jesus Christ, even we have believed in Christ Jesus that we may be justified by faith in Christ and not by works of the law, because by works of the law no one will be justified"*** (Galatians 1:16). The cry of the truly justified sinner is that he is ***"...justified freely by His grace through the redemption in Christ Jesus, Whom God set forth as an expiation, through faith, by His blood..."*** (Romans 3:24,25).

Only by belief in Christ's Gospel, which says a man is not saved based on anything he has done but solely by the grace of God through the election of grace, is a man saved: ***"...God chose you as the firstfruits for salvation through sanctification by the Spirit and belief in truth"*** (2 Thessalonians 2:13). ***"As He chose us in Him, before the foundation of the world, to be holy and without blemish before Him"*** (Ephesians 1:4); ***"He saved us and called us to a holy life, NOT ACCORDING TO OUR WORKS, but according to His own design and the grace bestowed on us in Christ Jesus before time began"*** (2 Timothy 1:9). No saved person ever came to God first (see 1 John 4:19). In every case God came to the person first and gave them the gift of salvation, not because they had in any way earned this gift, but freely and only by the will of God and the grace of God. Scripture says that by nature *"...there is no one who seeks God"* (Romans 3:11). *"But when one does not work, yet believes in the One Who justifies the ungodly, his faith is credited as righteousness. So also David declares the blessedness of the person to whom God credits righteousness apart from works"* (Romans 4:5,6).

Only by belief in Christ's Gospel, which says that Christ died exclusively for His people, those whom God had given Him (see John 17:2), and has provided them with an atonement for their sin, having their sins imputed, or charged, to Him and imputing unto them His perfect righteousness, is a man saved. Jesus said: *"I am the good shepherd. A good shepherd lays down His life for the sheep....I will lay down My life for the sheep"* (John 10:11,15). Writing to true believers Paul said, *"For our sake He made Him to be sin* (for us) *who did not know sin, so that we might become the righteousness of God in Him"* (2 Corinthians 5:21).

Only by belief in Christ's Gospel, which says that all His people shall come to Him, hear and believe His Gospel, is there true salvation. None whom the Lord has given unto Him shall perish, none shall be plucked from His Hand, but all for whom He died shall be saved: *"My sheep* *hear My voice; I know them, and they follow Me. I give them eternal life, and they shall never perish. No one can take them out of My hand"* (John 10:27,28). *"Everything that the Father gives Me WILL come to Me..."* (John 6:37).

Only by belief in Christ's Gospel, which states that none for whom He died shall ever perish, but all who have had their sins charged to Him shall be given eternal life, is a man saved. Salvation has not only been *obtained* for God's chosen, but it is eternally *maintained* by the Will of God and all that Christ has done: ***"...Give glory to Your Son, so that Your Son may glorify You, just as You gave Him authority over all people, so that He may give eternal life to all You gave Him"*** (John 17:1,2). Christ has not only obtained salvation for His people, by paying the penalty for their sin and imputing to them His righteousness, He also maintains their salvation by His eternal and completed work upon the cross. Thus ALL the glory for salvation belongs to God and none of it is shared with any man based on his works. **Only THIS Gospel gives ALL the glory to God for salvation and wherein there is no room for man to boast in anything he is or has done.**

Only by belief in Christ's Gospel, which states that no man is, or can be saved by his own righteousness, by his own efforts at obedience to God's Law, but only by the perfect Righteousness of Jesus Christ which is freely imputed based on His grace and mercy ALONE to all those for whom

He died, is a man saved. The apostle Paul wanted to *"...be found in Him, not having any righteousness of my own based on the law but that which comes through faith in Christ, the righteousness from God, depending on faith..."* (Philippians 3:9). Paul considered all that he was and did in the realm of religion as rubbish, **and therefore himself as a lost person,** before knowing Christ and His Gospel: *"...because of the supreme good of knowing Christ Jesus my Lord. For His sake I have accepted the loss of all things and I consider them so much rubbish..."* (Philippians 3:8).

Only those who have heard the Word of Truth, God's Mighty Gospel, can be said to truly hope in the true Christ: *"In Him you also, who have heard the word of truth, THE GOSPEL OF YOUR SALVATION, and have believed in Him, were sealed with the promised Holy Spirit"* (Ephesians 1:13).

Look then to the only true Jesus Who is the Author and Finisher of the Faith which God gives and which only believes in the true Gospel.

ANY AND ALL FAITH IN ANOTHER JESUS WILL NOT SAVE.

ANY AND ALL FAITH IN ANOTHER GOSPEL WILL NOT SAVE.

"Whoever believes (THE Gospel) *and is baptized will be saved; whoever does not believe will be condemned"* (Mark 16:16).

The true born again believer knows that **"...by grace you have been saved through faith, and this is not from you; it is the gift of God; it is not from works, so no one may boast"** (Ephesians 2:8,9).

May God bless each and every one of you with His Truth as revealed in His Gospel.

<u>NOTES</u>

[1] Roman Catholic Catechism, p.29, 1937 Australian Catholic Truth Society.

[2] Roman Catholicism, L. Boettner, p.220, 1962, Presbyterian and Reformed Publishing Co.

[3] The Catholic Encyclopaedia, Vol.7, p.783, article 'Indulgences'.

[4] Roman Catholicism, op.cit., p.219.

[5] Roman Catholic Catechism, op.cit., p.53.

[6] Babylon Mystery Religion: Ancient and Modern, R.E. Woodrow, p.61, 1966, R. Woodrow Evangelistic Association, Inc.

[7] Roman Catholic Catechism, op.cit., p.54.

[8] Systematic Theology, Vol.3, Dr. C. Hodge, p.770.

[9] Babylon Mystery Religion, op.cit., p.65.

[10] Roman Catholic Catechism, op.cit., p.29.

[11] Roman Catholic Catechism, ibid, p.29.

[12] Man and His gods, H.W. Smith, p.127, 1953, Boston: Little, Brown and Co.

[13] Roman Catholicism, op.cit., p.229

[14] 50 Years in the "Church" of Rome, C. Chiniquy, p.189, 1985, Chick Publications.

[15] Fundamental Protestant Doctrines (booklet), Dr. L.R. Harris, p.7.

[16] Roman Catholicism, op.cit.,.p 228.

[17] You Can Lead Roman Catholics To Christ, W. Ewin, p.109, 1961.

[18] Roman Catholicism, op.cit., p.225.

[19] Roman Catholicism, ibid, p.227.

[20] The Catholic Bible Has The Answer (booklet), O.J. Smith.

Please Contact:

morenodalbello@yahoo.com.au

Please Visit:

www.godsonlygospel.com

Made in the USA
Monee, IL
07 July 2026